HADLEIGH HOUSE PUBLISHING

Hadleigh House Publishing is a creative publishing house based in Minneapolis, Minnesota. Founded by two best-selling female authors, Hadleigh House is a collaborative place where authors work together and share in the success, investment and process of bringing a manuscript to the marketplace.

Founder Allison Mann, Hadleigh House, and the author and illustrator of this book are thrilled to back this project 100% in full and are donating all proceeds and royalties back into the non-profit: The Free Book Buggie.

For kids everywhere who are
currently dreaming up the ideas that are going to change the world.

And for Harper Colleen, remember that anything is possible if you dream big enough and work hard enough.

-Jen Teschendorf

Hadleigh House Publishing
Minneapolis, MN
www.hadleighhouse.com

The Free Book Buggie
Text and Design © 2022, by Jen Teschendorf
Cover and Interior Art © 2022, by Kevin Cannon
This is a work of fiction based on a non-profit organization of the same name.

All rights reserved.

No part of this book may be reproduced or transmitted in any form or by any means, electronic or mechanical, including photocopying, recording, or by any information storage or retrieval system, permitted by law. For information contact Hadleigh House Publishing, Minneapolis, MN.

ISBN: 978-1-7357738-9-6
LCCN: 2022943419

THE FREE BOOK BUGGIE

written by **Jen Teschendorf**
illustrated by **Kevin Cannon**

It started with a mom
who had an idea.

That idea began to grow.

It got bigger and bigger until one day...

...it grew so big that it transformed from an idea into a dream!

That dream was that every child could have access to free books.

IDEA: "the FREE BOOK BUGGIE!"

From chapter books, to picture books, to young adult books. Books that could make you laugh, or books that could make you cry. Books with bright colors or no colors at all. Books that talked about ducks, or dungeons, or doctors!

No matter what the genre, she wanted a place where kids could have access to any book they'd like.

Well, that dream began to grow. It got bigger and bigger until one day it grew so big, that it transformed from a dream into a garage!

That garage would collect books to give away to the kids who needed them.

People from the neighborhood heard about the idea that became a dream, so they started donating books to fill the garage.

Old books were given new life. Books that had been forgotten about, found new homes. There were books about gorillas, and gargoyles, and glitter! Books that had been read hundreds of times, and books that had only been read once.

The mom was overwhemed with gratitude from the community donations.

Well, that garage began to grow. It got bigger and bigger until one day it grew so big, that it transformed from a garage into a classroom! That classroom would turn into the new headquarters for all the book donations from the community.

Local thrift stores and organizations heard about the idea that became a dream, that started in a garage, that moved into a classroom. They started donating thousands of books a week.

There were books about cats, and China, and castles! Books that had puzzles and books that had answers. As the classroom filled with books, the students at the school began to volunteer.

Well, that classroom began to grow. It got bigger and bigger until one day it grew so big that it transformed from a classroom into a van! That van would be able to bring the books to the kids who needed them.

Pretty soon, the mom who once had an idea that became a dream took the books that the people donated from the classroom (that started in a garage) and moved them into a van.

She started to drive.

She went to events, met with kids and shared her books with the community. Kids chose books that looked special to them. They picked out books about violins, and vampires, and video games. Books that smelled old and books that smelled new.

Kids read books that gave them ideas that would one day turn into their own dreams!

Well, that van began to grow. It got bigger and bigger until one day it grew so big that it transformed from a van into a bus!

THE FREE BOOK BUGGIE

That bus would become The Free Book Buggie that would travel all around, making sure that every child could have access to free books.

Today, the mom who once had an idea that became a dream (that started in a garage, that moved to a classroom, that transformed into a van) now drives The Free Book Buggie all around town. She delivers books to Little Free Libraries, schools, and parks. She delivers books about trains, and tigers, and trumpets. Books that are big and books that are small.

Kids who had never been given a book suddenly have books of their very own.

Well, The Free Book Buggie began to grow...

Hi! I'm Debbie Beck, the founder of The Free Book Buggie.

When I was a child, my grandmother used to take us to the library, and I could never bring home enough books. I was the kind of child who could read for hours just immersing myself in that world. To this day I enjoy reading.

As an adult, I was a volunteer for my kids' school while they were growing up. For 11 years, I ran an I Love to Read month program. One of the events in the program was a book swap with the goal of each child having a book to take home. Children were encouraged to bring in books so they could exchange them and take home other books.

I was 50 years old when I enrolled at Metro State and completed my Master of Public and Nonprofit Administration while working full time and raising two children. The next few pages will talk about how The Free Book Buggie came to be, and the amazing team I have behind me making it happen.

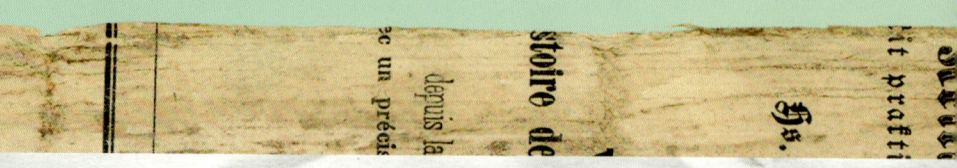

In 2018 I was on a trip with my daughter in Brazil. We walked into an outdoor park that had a colorful Volkswagen bus with all the doors open; filled with books for all to enjoy.

I had never seen anything like this. I grabbed my daughter's arm and said, "I know what I'm doing when I get home."

We sat down in the park with a tiny notebook and started dreaming of names for this project immediately.

On June 1, 2018, The Free Book Buggie was incorporated with the State of Minnesota as a nonprofit.

We operated out of my garage for only a of couple months before we quickly outgrew that space.

We moved into a friend's larger garage, then into an outdoor storage unit, and finally, in 2021, we moved our headquarters into Burnsville High School.

Our first year, we gave out 20,000 books.

The 2nd year was about 70,000.

Now after 4 years we have given out 270,000 books in communities in the Twin Cities.

Allison Mann

About the Publisher

Allison Mann is an author, publisher, and paralegal. After graduating from Winona State University in 2001, Allison began a nearly twenty-year career as a paralegal in the Twin Cities.

After co-authoring her first book, The Girls Are Gone, Allison found her way to the publishing world. In 2020, Allison co-founded and is the CEO of Hadleigh House Publishing.

Allison continues to reside in the Twin Cities with her family, enjoying life as a boy mom and all that comes along with it. When she's not writing, Allison can be found getting lost in a bookstore or wandering the halls of a courthouse.

About the Author

Jen Teschendorf lives in the Twin Cities with her husband, daughter, and their beloved dog, Rudy. She attended the University of Montana with the aspirations of learning how to make movies, but left with the artistry of telling a great story.

Jen typically can be found writing children's books, editing photos, or making short movies - but only after her little duck goes to sleep! Jen was recently elected to the Board of Directors on The Free Book Buggie and can't wait to help grow their mission and outreach.

Jen Teschendorf

Kevin Cannon

About the Illustrator

Kevin Cannon is an award-winning cartoonist and illustrator whose work has appeared in books, magazines, and games around the world. Recently Cannon was honored to be chosen as the button artist for the 2022 Saint Paul Winter Carnival and the commemorative poster artist for the 2021 Minnesota State Fair.

Cannon has illustrated over twenty children's books and numerous graphic novels, including the critically acclaimed Cartoon Introduction to Philosophy (Hill & Wang, 2015). This book has been translated into a dozen languages!

Cannon is thrilled to lend his talents to The Free Book Buggie and to help its mission to deliver books to children everywhere.

4. This is my cat named Cottleston Pie. She's the only cat in the world I'm not allergic to.

Fun Facts from Kevin!

1. I like to hide little pictures of my family in my projects. I even hid us in this book!

2. Pirates were my favorite thing to draw as a kid!

3. Early in my career I got to design (and help build) a family fun center in Wisconsin.

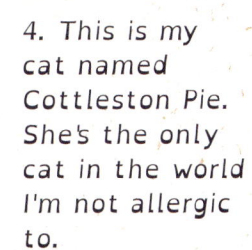

What is Dyslexic Inclusive font?

This book uses a dyslexic inclusive font that is enjoyable for everyone!

Author Jen Teschendorf first discovered this font when her original book, "Say What, Little Duck?" was picked up by a publishing company that created books for people with Dyslexia. Her book was re-printed in a dyslexic inclusive edition and can be found in bookstores and online!

Since then, Jen has been passionate about sharing her knowledge of Dyslexic Inclusive fonts with others! This book is printed in the dyslexia-friendly font called OpenDyslexic.

OpenDyslexic is an open-sourced font created to increase readability for readers with dyslexia. OpenDyslexic is created to help with some of the symptoms of dyslexia.

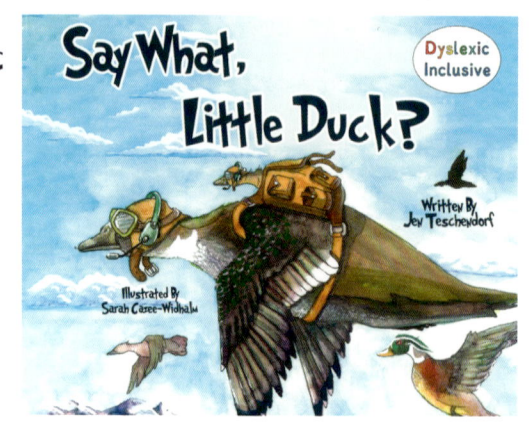

Letters have heavy-weighted bottoms to indicate direction. It helps readers to figure out which part of the letter is down, which helps in recognizing the correct letter, and can help to keep the brain from rotating them around. Additionally, OpenDyslexic uses unique letter shapes, to help prevent confusion.

Consistently weighted bottoms can also help reinforce the line of text. The unique shapes of each letter can help prevent confusion through flipping and swapping. A heavier bottom is used to show which way is supposed to be down.

Learn more and get the font at www.opendyslexic.org